The Love Life Of A College Student

Chynna Krouser

BookLeaf Publishing

India | USA | UK

Presentation by *BookLeaf Publishing*

Web: www.bookleafpub.com

E-mail: info@bookleafpub.com

ISBN: 9789360943059

First edition 2024

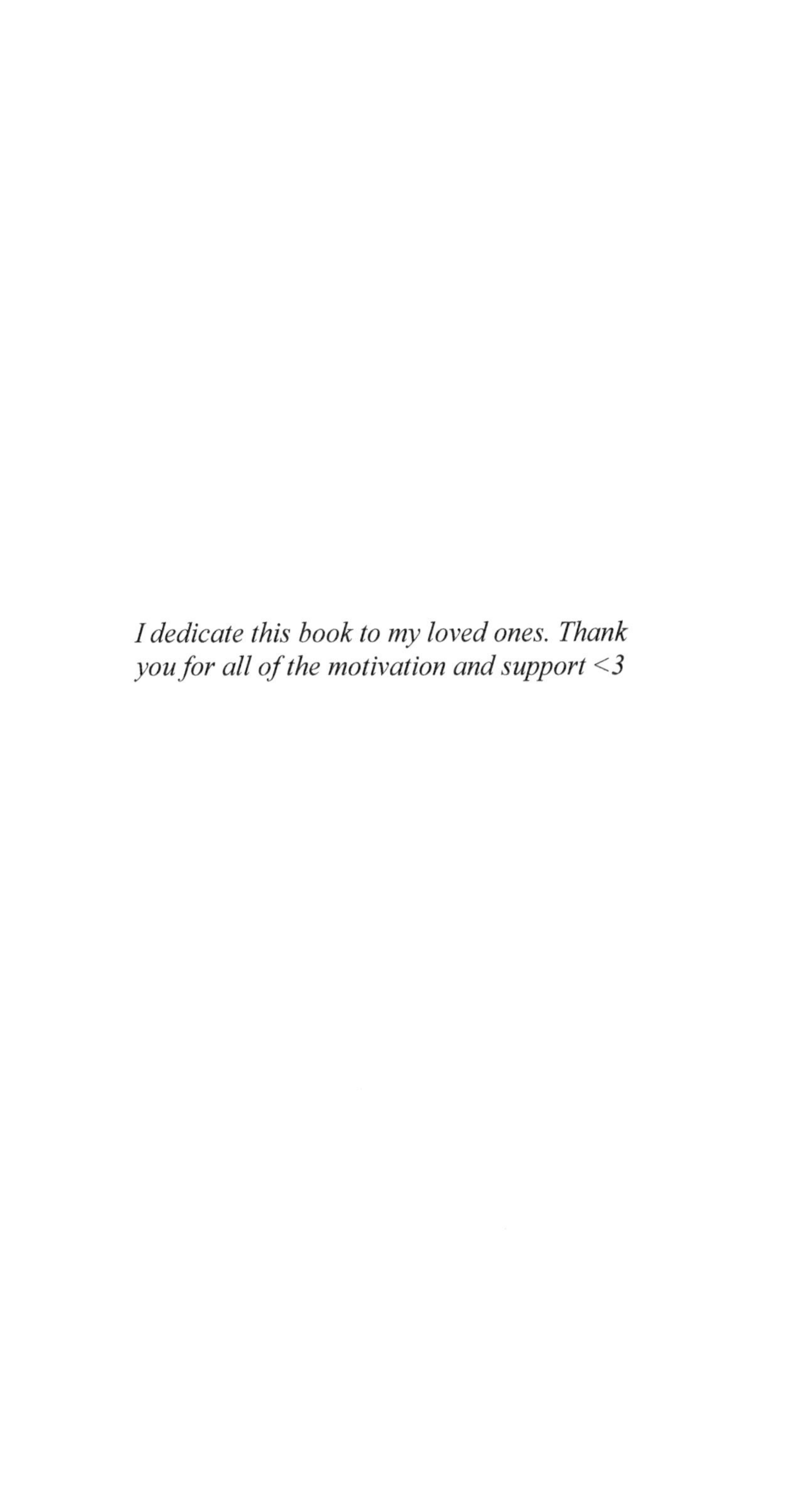

I dedicate this book to my loved ones. Thank you for all of the motivation and support <3

How Can I Describe My Life To You

After Susan Sontag and
@betweenthelinesandspaces

I smile a lot. Even on the days where there's nothing to smile about. I take a picture of every pretty flower I see, tickle my cheeks with the petals. Catch floating feathers and turn them into wishes. Pray to the moon and shout at the stars. Jump of swings. Get roadrash in the sprinklers. Do too much and not enough. I wear blush on my nose. Throw up peace signs whenever a camera sees me. Take things too seriously. Cry any time a dog is in a movie. Or any time there's a really good love story. Always need a blanket. And cuddles. I love a hot cocoa in the winter. Laugh when the whipped cream sticks to my nose.

Recipe Of My Brain

Ingredients:

-3 pounds of gray matter
-6 cups of doubt
-Several tablespoons of anxiety
-2 8oz Jars of Hope
-½ cup of overthinking
-1 6oz can of thoughtfulness
-3 cups of love
-A bushel of nice n' sweet
-Grounded motivation (garnish)

Instructions:

1. Place 3 pounds of gray matter in a bowl.
2. Add the 6oz can of thoughtfulness.
3. Add 6 cups of love, you should have the extra 3 cups lying around somewhere. Knead to mix.
4. Chop the bushel of nice n' sweet to your liking. Add to bowl. (Don't put too much or results may be naive.)

5. Add ½ cup of overthinking. Knead until thoroughly homogenized. Then knead a little more.

6. Add the 2 jars of hope. Make sure they're whole pieces, you don't want them chunked.

7. Add a few tablespoons of anxiety. It's best to eyeball it.

8. Add a sprinkle of doubt, be careful not to add too much.

9. Empty contents of bowl onto baking sheet, shape into a loaf. Bake at 98.6 degrees F for 9 hours. Plate when done.

10. Add some ground motivation on top for garnish. Or don't.

Snail Mail

What to write in a letter?
Boasting about amazing things seems
pretentious. Listing angry and sad is
depressing. But otherwise I'm boring.
How are you? Tell me about everything that
has made you angry or sad. I can give
you advice or be here to vent.
Tell me all the amazing things going on
in your life. It's ok, I won't be jealous!
Tell me your fears and ambitions.
Do you believe in aliens?
Tell me
Tell me
Tell me more

Plums

5

You asked me "what's your favorite fruit?"

We sat at the large weeping willow tree. The one we always sat at as kids. You held a burlap sack of plums, the thin straps rested daintily on your shoulder. The warm summer breeze lifted your dark hair into sunlit golden strands. Your slender fingers reached to get a plum. The juice dripped down your chin as you sank your teeth into purple flesh.

And in that moment, I said plums. After all, they were your favorite. And that's all the reason I needed.

Black Ball Bracelet

Small
Shiny
Round black beads.
Two yank the Peach fuzz on my wrist,
a fire burns up my arm,
snaps me out of my thoughts.
The reminder of a broken heart
rising from the ashes.
You gave me this bracelet
It pinches me to remind me
that I'm real,
that this all isn't just a dream.
You always taught me that
life is painful but worth living.

The Quad

I look at her from
across the courtyard.
The sun hits her dark
Brown hair just right,
Casting golden-light brown
Shimmers down her face.
If she spoke to me
From where she sat,
The song would travel
Perfectly to my right eardrum.
Her eyes are dark and
Ever-changing
As she stares at the rowboat
On the river.
There could never be a
Dull moment in her world.
But her eyes don't flutter
Back towards me.
Because I'm boring.

Otherside Of The Quad

I see his glances,
but can't bring myself
to meet his eyes.
My friend is talking,
But I can only concentrate
on the way the wind
ruffles his golden hair.
Even with a fountain between us,
and the sun in my eyes,
I can easily spot him.
To touch him would be as
sweet as chocolate melting
on my tongue.
But, I do not belong
in his presence.
I stare out at a rowboat on the river,
continue to nod at
my friend's gibberish,
anything to distract myself
from him.
I'm just not his type.

Astronomy 101

9

What's the point in studying astronomy
When the only thing I need from the
Stars is to tell me if you'll stay?
With me.
To see if we're compatible on a
Mental
Emotional
Physical
Spiritual
Level?

Biology

Be with me
In all the chaos
Of
Life's journey, as
Organisms
Genetically predisposed to
Yearning.

Physics 102

Electricity moves through the positives and
negatives of my veins with the
Potential to
Work through the ups and downs of something
in the
Distance.
Examples of larger
Problems to come that we attempt to
Draw through
Diagrams keep heading our way. But these
Sketches are only of
Flowers. Our
Opposite traits
Charge our attraction, but won't make this
Absolute. The rules of physics aren't always
Relative. Yet, I still feel your heart
Pulling towards mine, and all the problems just
become
Numbers. It seems we only get
Halfway when we feel filled to
Capacity. But what would we be if we let that
define our
Quest? How would we know the
Difference? Are we in
Series? Or are we

Parallel? The
Voltage is too strong when we're
Combined. How will we stop this from getting
Boring?

Geology

I'm so shakey.
Fingers earthquakes
sending tremors down my spine.
Aftershocks into my stomach.

They go silent at your touch.
My volcanoes no longer erupting,
pouring into their next victims.
My tsunamis no longer threatening to
swallow the land.

Living Parts

14

They say
that parts of the
people we used to
love still remain inside of
us after they are gone.

I hope you can
find a way to
love the parts of
them that still live within
me.

Pieces of Myself

15

I buy you my favorite books,

I show you quotes from
my favorite shows,
and clips from
my favorite movies.

I make playlists for you
from my favorite songs.

And this is how I give you
pieces of myself.

Normal People

"I'm not a religious person but I do sometimes
think God made you for me." - Normal People
by Sally Rooney

And maybe,
Somehow,
God made too much of
"Me" elixir,
and had to use the extras
on someone else.
And maybe
that is how we
came to be
soul-mates.

Beginning Of The End

And after 3 months,
you have already stopped:

Texting me goodnight

Holding my hand

Answering my calls

Drawing finger circles across my thighs

Making time to hang out

Planning dates (yes, they're different.)

Keeping promises

Showing effort

Remembering birthdays

Honoring plans

Being actionable

Saying what you mean
&
Meaning what you say

Flip-Flop

19

Fickle.
The way your head sways
in the breeze.
You never had to make a decision,
so why start now?
Capricious,
I can wear you on my feet
at the beach,
and let the sun cooked sand
warm my toes.

Prosthetic Heart

20

Does plastic feel pain?
If not,
Then can it take mine?
Can it cure the earthquakes
of my mind or
rid the hurricanes in my blood?
Can it fix whole the broken
trust in my heart,
or make it new?

I Always Give Plant Seeds
As Parting Gifts

To exes,
old friends.
After a few years,
they always tell me how well
they have kept up.
How they were able to water
and care for them.

Unlike our relationship.

They always seem to
be able to keep their gardens
blooming, just to prove that
the grass is always greener
on their side

when they want it to be.

My World

22

My world
doesn't revolve
around you. But when you
left, my world definitely stopped
spinning.

The Life Cycle Of A Butterfly

Larvae (11-18 days):

I was a small child in preschool the first time I learned about the life cycle of a butterfly. It was early spring when Ms. Cathy brought out the caterpillar larvae. We prepped by reading The Very Hungry Caterpillar by Eric Carle. Every day, we would go outside in the brisk spring air to collect fresh leaves, and every day we excitedly circled around the caterpillars' enclosure, all of us dropping the brightest, greenest leaves to feed our new friends. They really started to feel at home in our classroom.

Chrysalis (8-14 days):

We watched as our class pets embedded themselves into a cocoon (something I also wanted to do, even at that young age). We were told that the chrysalis was like a home that a caterpillar builds around itself so it can continue growing. We couldn't wait for our friends to come out. They were missing so much that was going on in the classroom, after all. I would peak

in every day, watching the chrysalis colors
change from lime green to deep green to clear. I
imagined having a butterfly sanctuary in our
classroom, growing a garden. I was beyond
excited. I wasn't aware of what would happen
next.

Adult (22+ days):

We watched as the butterflies emerged, slowly
taking steps out of their temporary home,
stretching and fluttering their wings. It was
beautiful. All this time had led up to this
moment. Ms. Cathy showed us how to give them
sugar water, lightly soaking a cotton ball and
hanging it in the enclosure. The next day, we
went out again, looking for fresh leaves and
flowers for our butterflies' home. Ms. Cathy
brought them with us this time. We circled
around their netted enclosure, speculating about
the best colored flowers to collect.
The zipper was opened.
The butterflies flew out.
They flew higher,
higher,
higher.
My head followed them until my eyes burned
from the sun's rays. They did not fly back into

the enclosure. They did not come back. They were gone.
I cried.

This was when I first learned:

I have trouble letting go.

The Half-Life of Love is Forever

The Half-Life of love is forever
And no Junot Diaz could ever explain
That no matter the duration
It's all the same pain

Because you've gone through

so much together.

You cry every time
you hear their favorite song.

Everyone asks if you're ok
and you always say you're fine

but you're not.

You write them (pathetic) letters
in hopes you'll get the guts
to send any of them

                              As if

it'll change their mind.

                                    But it
won't.

                                    So you
don't send any.

Then there's the depression
The feeling of slowly being taken apart.
When you look into the mirror,
yet can't look at yourself as a whole
                                    'Cause
that part of you is

Missing.

The feeling that someone flew
a plane into your soul.
                                    Or
maybe two.

Then there's the
(ridiculous) hope
that they'll come back to you

                                    or
forgive you.
                                    But that
won't happen.
You get the courage
to delete all the pictures,
all the memories

                                    and say
goodbye for good.
                                    (But
will it work?)

You try to start over,
                                    begin a
new slate,
and when you do
you feel lighter.
                    So you start dating.

You start getting places,
meeting new people,
                                    But no
one like your ex.

You finally meet someone,
                                    and
you're happy
                                    (for the
first time in how long?)
Someone in the same
place you are.
And though you like them,
it all feels too
                                    lacking
in promise.
But, you know it takes time.

(Hey, didn't the last one?)

                                        So, you
try to be patient.

But it doesn't turn out well.
And even these other breakups suck

                                        No
matter how small the pain

                                        because
you're back to thinking

of the ex.

So you focus on yourself for awhile.
You find new things to do

                                        to keep
yourself from thinking of them.

            It's your new addiction.

But you think of them anyways.
And when you try to talk,

                                        they
don't answer.

And it scares you
because you don't want to

                                        go back
under.

                                             go back
into the depression.

You peel away from others
                                             like

you're ashamed of yourself.
You hate the ex
for being without you,

but you're happy
knowing they're happy
                                             so you

try to bury the hate.

                              Yet, the revenge is
living well
                              without you.

You don't hang around
your old friends,
                                             'cause

they'll only talk about the ex.

But you still find yourself
dreaming about them.
You want the old times back,
where they would talk to you;
touch you

                                              but you
know you can't.

You keep calling them,
trying to get them to talk.
                                              Even

say something stupid
                                              just to

get a reaction
but realize that maybe that's
why they won't talk.

                       You're stuck in a loop.

A loop where you're
waiting to stop

thinking of them.
How long could it take
to get over them?
                                              people
say one year,
                                              maybe

two.
But you know you'll never
get over it.
No matter the will power.
                                              You

just have to accept that it's over.

So, you still have dreams
of the ex.
And you re-write their name
for the millionth time
on a page

                                              that

says The Half-Life of Love is Forever.

And, you go on
starting something new
because sometimes

                                    a start is all we

ever get.